I0454212

Abramović-isms

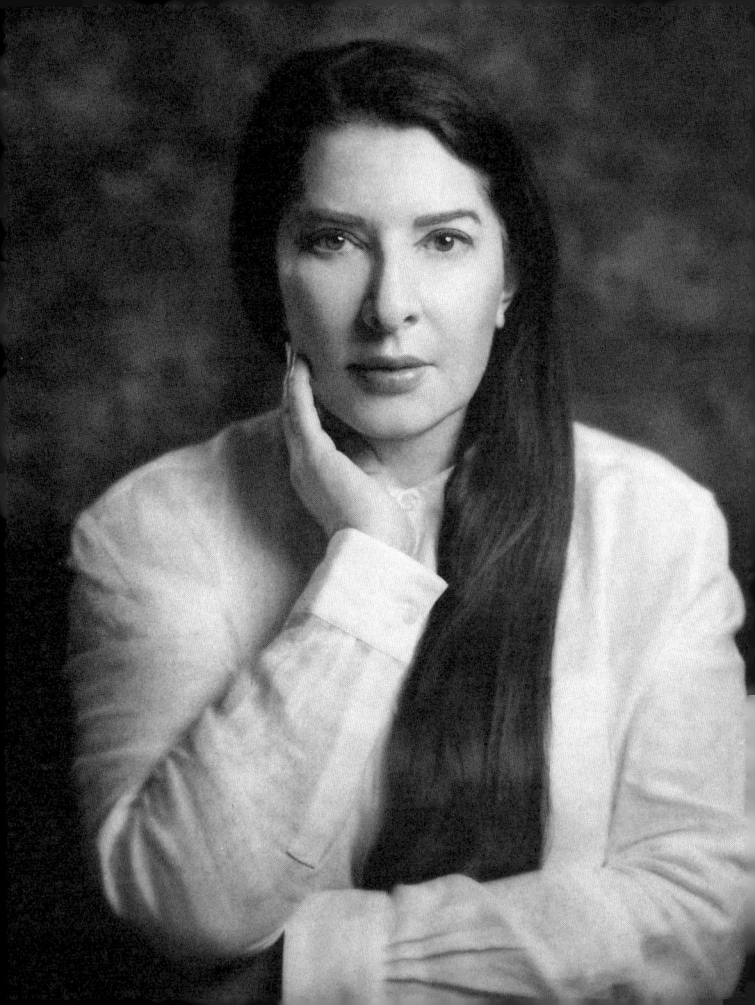

Abramović-isms

Marina Abramović

Edited by Larry Warsh

PRINCETON UNIVERSITY PRESS
Princeton and Oxford

in association with
No More Rulers

Copyright © 2024 by LW Archives, LLC
Marina Abramović quotations © Marina Abramović

Princeton University Press is committed to the protection of
copyright and the intellectual property our authors entrust to us.
Copyright promotes the progress and integrity of knowledge.
Thank you for supporting free speech and the global exchange
of ideas by purchasing an authorized edition of this book.
If you wish to reproduce or distribute any part of it
in any form, please obtain permission.

Requests for permission to reproduce material from this work
should be sent to permissions@press.princeton.edu

Published by Princeton University Press,
41 William Street, Princeton, New Jersey 08540

In the United Kingdom: Princeton University Press,
99 Banbury Road, Oxford OX2 6JX
press.princeton.edu
in association with
No More Rulers
nomorerulers.com
ISMs is a trademark of No More Rulers, Inc.

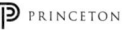 PRINCETON NO MORE RULERS ®

All Rights Reserved
ISBN 9780691263731
Library of Congress Control Number: 2024933242
British Library Cataloging-in-Publication Data is available

This book has been composed in Johanna MT
Printed in China
1 3 5 7 9 10 8 6 4 2

CONTENTS

INTRODUCTION

Warrior. Shaman. Revolutionary. Artist.

Those words spring to mind when I think of Marina Abramović. Her exploration of the human experience—and of the body as a tool for artistic expression—is utterly fearless and subversive. She is no stranger to pain, mental or physical. For her, suffering is a catalyst, a constant source of creativity, pushing her work to new levels. In Marina's art, performance is transformation. Her works deconstruct the illusion of time and carry us into a transcendent state. She draws energy from her audiences, turns it into strength, and creates an experience through tremendous willpower and concentration. Through her discipline and unflinching drive for discovery, Marina has created a body of work that defies categorization.

The quotations excerpted in this volume are gathered from a range of articles, interviews, and discussions. They delve into the mind of this visionary thinker, exploring her artistic processes, her spirituality, influences, and core beliefs.

For Marina's first major work, *Rhythm 10* (1973), she positioned herself before ten knives and placed her left hand on white paper, rhythmically stabbing at the spaces between her fingers until she accidentally wounded herself. At that point she would take a new knife and start again; the performance ended once she cut herself twenty times. This work initiated the Rhythm series, five performance works that focused on her body as art and object, testing her physical and mental limitations. The series culminated in *Rhythm 0* (1974), a six-hour performance in which Marina laid out seventy-two objects and posted a statement on the wall declaring,

"I am the object. During this period I take full responsibility."[1] Though the audience interactions were initially mild, over time her clothes were torn off, her neck was cut with a razor blade, and one participant placed a loaded pistol in her hand and aimed it at her head.

Transformation is key to Marina for both herself and her audience, and endurance is part of her DNA. Perhaps her most renowned work is *The Artist Is Present* (2010). Performed as part of a major Abramović retrospective at the Museum of Modern Art in New York, the piece consisted of the artist sitting in a chair and wordlessly locking eyes, one by one, with a succession of visitors in the seat across from her. The work ran every day, eight hours a day, for nearly three months. Among the participating visitors was Ulay, whom Marina had not seen since 1988.

Though Marina began creating her work on

the fringes of the art world, her creative rigor and original thinking have made her an internationally celebrated figure, and she continues to inspire an incisive reconsideration of the meaning and purpose of art. In a society and an art world focused on material success, Marina has fundamentally changed the way we understand creative expression. Through the quotations in this book—assembled with the artist's input—I hope to shed new light on the universes within her mind and to illuminate her words as tools of creative and spiritual connection.

LARRY WARSH
NEW YORK CITY
JANUARY 2024

1 Marina Abramović, Rhythm 0, Tate, https://www.tate.org.uk/art/artworks/abramovic-rhythm-0-t14875.

Early Years
and Family Stories

My father and mother came from totally different backgrounds. My mother was from a very rich family and had studied in Switzerland; my father was one of 17 children, incredibly poor, and had been in prison before the war for his politics. So he was pure Communist, my mother was pure bourgeois, and they clashed so much. Everything was about willpower. (9)

———

I come from [the former] Yugoslavia—in my country black humor is very important. You need to laugh, even if there's nothing to laugh about. (16)

———

When I was a child, my father and mother
would be very violent to each other, and
every time they would raise their
voices I would just freeze. (14)

———

The brother of my grandfather was the
patriarch of the Orthodox Church and revered
as a saint. So everything in my childhood is
about total sacrifice, whether to religion or to
Communism. This is what is engraved on me.
This is why I have this insane willpower. (2)

———

With my mother, it was incredible discipline and order. When she was pregnant with me, she dreamt that she was giving birth to a huge snake. She was at a Party meeting when her waters broke, but she didn't want to leave the meeting until it was finished, because she was presiding, and so she was taken to the hospital in emergency. And then I was taken straight to [her mother] and I spent my first six years with her. (9)

I saw my mother and father just as these
strange guys who came to bring me
presents—and I never wanted any of their
presents. I didn't like dolls, I played only
with shadows—I was strange from
the beginning. (9)

———

My grandmother spent most of the time
in church, from morning till evening. She
was deeply religious, and she deeply hated
Communism. With her, it was all about silence
and ritual. Her mysticism really is very strong
in my work. I would never be what I am if
I didn't have this mixture. (9)

———

My mother always used to give me sets of instructions for what I should achieve every day—to learn a certain number of French words, for example, or what I should eat, what kind of books I should read, what time I was supposed to be home. That time of my life was based in a frame of discipline. (23)

———

I stayed at home until I was 29. I could only do performances before 10 in the evening, because I had to be home by then. So, all this burning myself, cutting my stomach, whatever, I had to do before 10! (9)

———

I was like a black sheep, I was constantly
trying to rebel. Both my mother and father
were [censured] by Party meetings for my
upbringing: How could I do this kind of stuff?
It was for the mental hospital, not for art!
So, that really made me strong. (9)

—

When I was six, seven, I was drawing
everywhere, on the walls, the sheets … And
my mother really supported this activity,
because she was the director of the Museum
of the Revolution and Art in Belgrade. I would
go with her all the time, so I was exposed to
art and I was always thinking of El Greco,
things like that. So, I have to give her that. (9)

—

I sent [my mother] my books—I have made 46 books, really big ones, like 300, 400 pages—and when she died I looked at them and I could not believe it. All of them were like 35, 45 pages. Every photo [in which] I was naked, she just tore it out—she wouldn't show it to the neighbors! (9)

———

When I left Yugoslavia I was 29 years old and I literally escaped. Until then, all my performances were very difficult and physically and mentally consuming. ... When I eventually escaped, [my mother] went to the police to announce my disappearance, and the police asked, "How old is she?" and when she said, "29," they said: "It's about time." (10)

———

Career Path

I realized at a very early stage that my purpose was to be an artist. The first thing I did was painting my dreams: I was twelve years old and I was very jealous of Mozart because he had started his career when he was seven. (8)

———

If I think in my gut that I'm right, I do it. you have to have this kind of conviction. Otherwise, I would have given up many years ago. (1)

———

Artists suffer a lot in their life. Nobody make[s] anything from happiness. (17)

———

When I was very young I went to see the most difficult operation that can be done to a human, which was the replacement of the hip and spine. The operation lasted between three to five hours. They use saw machines, screws and metal, to cut the body into pieces and then put it back together again. This was pretty fascinating to me and so I decided I wanted to experiment with pushing the body to its limits, exploring how I deal with pain.

(22)

———

I struggled with acceptance; my early career was hell. But it took me all these years to create a foundation so that performance would become accepted in the same way as photography and video. (1)

———

In one of my first shows, all my photographs sold, but I never got a penny. (1)

———

The end of the 1970s was somehow the end of performance art—the galleries, the dealers, the museums—they just could not actually deal with something that was so immaterial like performance. There was nothing to sell and there was real pressure on artists in those times to create objects, to create paintings, to create—you know—things. (10)

———

At the end of the 1970s, my generation of performance artists—from Chris Burden and Dennis Oppenheim to Gina Pane and Vito Acconci—had stopped performing. They were making objects or dealing with architecture or painting, but not performance, whereas I felt that performance was far from over. I was looking for different ways to use the body and to push it beyond the limits of our culture. (10)

———

I'm so happy I didn't give up. (1)

———

I started looking at what is around me and using it for art. It took me just a little while to realize that I could be my art. (2)

———

I started painting clouds—I was always looking into the sky. One day, I was lying on the grass and there came maybe 12 supersonic fighter planes and they create this incredible drawing in the sky, and I have a revelation. I say: "This is incredible! Why should I do something two-dimensional when I can use everything? I can use fire, I can use water, I can use the sky. I can use my body." (9)

———

I gradually started involving the body—and as soon as I started using my body it changed everything. (9)

———

I got involved with performance after making sound installations. At one point, I started using my body, and then, I never could go back into the seclusion of the studio and just make objects or other types of artwork. Performance was something that fit my nature the best. (13)

———

In my 20s, 30s, and 40s I was criticized for my art, especially by men. Now in my 60s and 70s I am criticized by women. It is amazing that they think you are not supposed to look good and feel happy when you are 70. It is incredible how much hostility there is. (7)

———

People who love you start to hate you when you become that rock star. Everybody is scrutinizing. They want you to be poor, to suffer, to struggle. I could not pay my electricity bill until I was 50, and now I can. I think this is something I should not be criticized for. (1)

———

Rhythm 0 is a very interesting work because until then everybody was talking about how performance is not a form of art, it is all bullshit, you know, it's exhibitionism—the artist just wants to be naked. And there I was, completely dressed, beside 72 objects that could hurt me or give me pleasure and the public were completely free to do whatever they wanted. And what happened? It provoked a wild reaction. They only didn't rape me because they had come with their wives! I was just an object—It was amazing! I knew [then] that the public could kill me. (9)

———

I have made two pieces in my life that were most dangerous for me. The most interesting pieces, for me, are the ones where I'm not in control. In the one called Rhythm 0 the public was in control—they could do whatever they wanted with me. The other one was this piece [*Rest Energy*] (performed with Ulay in 1980) which was based on trust—if either of us lost control, the arrow would go straight into my heart. It was simple. We held the bow and arrow with our weight until we really could not hold it anymore. We had to release at the same time. (10)

———

I could never do this in my own private life, but if I stage the situation in front of an audience—and the staged situation is dangerous—I can take energy from the audience and use it to give me strength to go through that experience. So I become like your mirror. If I can do this in my life, you can do it in yours, and through that I liberate myself from fear. (10)

—————

You know, performance really has this kind of power to change not just the performer's life but also the one who is witnessing the performance. (10)

—————

This incredible miracle happened [during the performance of 512 *Hours* at the Serpentine Gallery]: people began to wake up with regard to who they were. The most moving part for me was that the public had the possibility to feel this energy. Two-hundred and fifty thousand people attended the show. This gave me a sense of purpose: the feeling that my performance may afford clarity, that it may awaken consciences. I only gave them the possibility to reconnect with themselves.

I find this really thrilling. (8)

————

With *The Artist Is Present*, the reaction of the public was very emotional. They cried, and really got in touch with their deeper self. In that performance, I isolated the public, one on one, but still within the group because anyone who sat in front of me was photographed, and filmed, and watched by me and watched by the wider audience, and there was nowhere to go except deeper into themselves[,] and when that happened, it was very emotional. I could [not] have done *The Artist Is Present* when I was young. I didn't have the experience, the willpower, concentration, or wisdom. I could only do it when I was 65. (22)

———

I've been looking by now into 1,565 pair of
eyes [during *The Artist Is Present*], which is lots
of eyes, and the people who I look [at],
I know them, they're like family. (21)

———

At first I was interested in the limits
of the body; now I focus on the limits
of the mind. (8)

———

Many think that my work is easier now, but
cutting oneself is actually not so difficult:
there is only a bit of blood. On the other
hand, penetrating into this unknown ocean
that is the mind, coming into contact with
the unconscious is really difficult. (8)

———

It is very hard to sustain a career of 55 years because you always have to be as curious as a child, reinvent yourself, and have the spirit of the time you are living in. (7)

———

Don't ever call me the grandmother of performance art. Just call me a warrior. (3)

———

The Personal as Political

Both my parents were war heroes in
[the former] Yugoslavia, and my entire
childhood I was taught that I had to sacrifice
my private life and everything else for the
cause. Why are you here on this planet? What
is your function? What is your responsibility?
That's how I was brought up, and
that's what I've been doing. (1)

———

When people ask me where I am from,
I never say Serbia. I always say I come from
a country that no longer exists. (2)

———

[My first performances in public were] short, intense political pieces where I am plunging the knife between my fingers and cutting the Communist star on my body. (2)

———

I give my complete support to Ukraine. People are dying, and in this kind of situation, we all—especially artists—have to be very strong with our voices. We all need to be on the same page, against this barbarian thing. Putin is a 19th-century brutalist. (3)

———

Ukraine can be Syria, anywhere. When you make the work and you make the message, you have to create something that is actually transcendental, that can be used in so many different ways, as the society needs at the time. (6)

———

Art can show the way. But there is not something else that can change you, every individual has to change themselves first. It's up to us. It's not that some kind of miraculous force will come and then everything will stop. We always put this responsibility somewhere else. Responsibility is us, ourselves, what we can do right now, today, to change something. (4)

———

Without even realizing it, we create so many
superstructures for ourselves and our society.
We are the only ones who can change them.
We can all be warriors in our own
unique way. (5)

———

I had a family that mixed both the
Orthodox religion and Communism, which
is conflicting in itself. I grew up in that
contradiction and my work expresses it best.
At that time, I was educated not to think about
my personal life. I was taught everything
that is important points towards a
higher purpose in your life. (7)

———

I don't believe in Gods or religion. I really believe in energy, in divine spirit. I believe in the kind of enlightenment where you experience a complete purification of your mind and body and you lift your spirit to another level. I saw it and experienced it myself so I really believe in it. (7)

———

The five-point star I cut on my stomach when I was in Yugoslavia was not the Jewish star, it was the Communist star. I was born with that star, it was on my birth certificate. It was on every book at school. It was in every celebration of Communism. It really was something that I felt that I wanted to get rid of, that symbol. (10)

———

I think political correctness has had a stifling effect on creativity. If you think about artists like the Futurists in the 1920s and 1930s, Dadaism, Surrealism, natural art, conceptual art, or performance art from the 1950s, 1960s, and 1970s, these people had incredible freedom of expression and the freedom to express their ideas. The things that were done at those times constituted a major chapter in the history of art, but some of them would be not possible today because of political correctness. (11)

———

I'm not interested in politics per se, although it cannot be denied that some of my pieces have political content. I'm more into the transcendental aspects of the work. You can transfer ideas and make changes in the observer's mind. (13)

———

I know it might sound like a strong statement, but I've always felt that an artist is a servant of society. If you have the gift of creativity, you have to share it because it doesn't belong to you only. And creativity should be removed from male and female specificity. (5)

———

To become a woman artist, you have to
sacrifice. You can't have this normal life like
people. It's lots of solitude, lots of lonely
haunted rooms, and you have to be
ready for that. (18)

———

I have no children and no husband. The truth
is that I am not a very good prospect. My
work is everything. Focusing completely on
my work is a solitary task. I have no
private life. I am the perfect example
of a modern nomad. (8)

———

I tried to have the marriage life, but it
didn't really work. I always felt guilty that
I worked and traveled too much. (1)

———

I didn't want children because I didn't want them to suffer. (1)

———

I have always been out of the box and I will always continue to be that way. (7)

———

Toxic masculine energy belongs to the past. The Hero is facing the future. It is important for art to find new avenues to engage with new audiences, especially now, otherwise we are all fucked. (4)

———

We are so much stronger, especially us women, because we have the power to create life. We seem weak but we have that incredible power so if we, voluntarily, play the role of being submissive, fragile and servants to men, it is because their love is very important to us. This is why I never say I am a feminist. Why should I? I already have the power. (7)

I make so many statements concerning women and feminism, in which I say, "I am female but I am an artist." I don't admit that artists have gender because I don't care who's making the art. The only thing that's important to me is whether it is good art or bad art. (22)

I think the function of the artist is to change the ways humans can think. The key role, like Duchamp or that kind of an artist thought, is to change the way that society thinks. The important thing is to find the point where society will change. (13)

———

Performance Art, the Body, and the Mind

Our body is an absolute replica of the Universe, and this is why I took to studying myself—by studying myself, I can understand everything else and everybody else. (15)

———

I have to start with myself because myself is what I know best. (5)

———

[The human brain] is one of the most ancient and complicated computers on the planet. (15)

———

We forgot about the wisdom of the body itself, which I think is really as old as our Milky Way, as old as the black holes in the Universe. I even think that the mind came later—the body came first. (15)

———

You have to train the entire body: training physically, thinking about nutrition, not taking drugs, not ever drinking. (1)

———

It takes years and years and years of practice to really learn how to listen to your own body— what it is telling you to do—and not to your mind. Because the mind is tricky. The mind can constantly lead you in the wrong direction as well as invent things that don't exist. (15)

———

The mind is a huge enemy because every time you try to do something out of your comfort zone, it will make you not do it. But we all have this extra energy in our body. We might use it when we're in extreme situations, trapped or in a plane crash or a fire, and we're able to run out. But we don't need to wait for this drama. (1)

———

You can really be completely delusional and live in a kind of "truth" that is actually false. But the physical, the body, is the wisdom that will absolutely never lie to you. And then we also have this enormous power of the body: healing, raising the body's temperature, slowing the heartbeat, you know—intuition, telepathy, all of this stuff. And the only thing we have to do is develop this. (15)

———

To me [performance art] is one of the hardest types of art, because it's immaterial, it's time based, it's very much to do with emotions and the public. (3)

———

For me, the long duration of a piece is the key
to real transformation—and performance art
is nothing without transformation. (2)

———

Performance can be seen in so many different
ways. Of course there's a therapeutic element.
I always believe that a good work
of art has to have many layers of meaning.
It can be political. It can be social.
It can be spiritual. It can predict the future.
There are so many different ways that
it can be taken by every person who
experiences it. (10)

———

To be a performance artist, you have to hate theater. Theater is fake. ... The knife is not real, the blood is not real, and the emotions are not real. Performance is just the opposite: the knife is real, the blood is real, and the emotions are real. (2)

———

I test the limits of myself in order to transform myself but I also take the energy from the audience and transform it. It goes back to them in a different way. This is why people in the audience often cry or become angry or whatever. A powerful performance will transform everyone in the room. (2)

My work is emotional, and I never hide anything. But it took me a long time to get to that point. (1)

———

To be able to sit on the chair in *The Artist Is Present*, I trained my body for an entire year. I didn't eat during the day, only by night, so my body wasn't producing acids to make me sick. I drank water only by night so I wouldn't have to pee. (1)

———

Physically, mentally, I [had] to prepare myself for a feat of endurance. I became a vegetarian, I did deep meditation, I cleansed myself. I train the body and the mind. I learn to eat certain foods so that I don't have to go to the toilet for seven hours. I learn to sleep in short bursts at night. This is very hard: sleep, wake, drink, pee, exercise, sleep, wake, and on and on. So even the not-performing is intense. (2)

———

[In *The Artist Is Present*], I give people a space to simply sit in silence and communicate with me deeply but nonverbally. I did almost nothing, but they take this religious experience from it. Art had lost that power, but for a while MoMA was like Lourdes. (2)

———

I become a mirror for them of their own emotions [during *The Artist Is Present*]. One big Hell's Angel with tattoos everywhere stared at me fiercely, but after 10 minutes was collapsing into tears and weeping like a baby.

(2)

———

Another thing that was for me very touching was that the [MoMA staff] who guarded the museum every day would come on their free day in civilian clothes and wait in the line to sit with me, because they wanted the experience. That's something that does not [normally] happen. (9)

———

I still have to make more works, and I always think something revolutionary will come out of me. But I can say [*The Artist Is Present*] was the most transformative work—this work transformed me into something else. Something happened there. It was that incredible discovery of unconditional love to any single person standing in front of me. (6)

―――

My body is now beginning to be falling apart, but I will do it to the end. I don't care. With me it is about whatever it takes. (2)

―――

I still look at my body as a machine and I still use the mind—the will—to control what I do but there is something more Buddhist now about the performances. (2)

———

In my first performance, I experienced my transformation immediately. I left behind my doubts and low self-esteem and discovered my higher self. When I perform, I feel beautiful, radiant, and powerful. Everything is possible, and the world around me becomes luminous.

(5)

———

As a performance artist, I need the attention and the energy from the public, and a way for me to achieve that is to stage my own fears, vulnerabilities, and pains so that the audience can relate to them. I don't think there's a part of myself that I haven't exposed, although there are definitely things that many people don't know about me. (5)

———

I do not rehearse my performances. I let life and energy go through it, and by that I mean that an earthquake can happen, someone in the audience faints, or the public interrupts the work. There is not a predetermined flow, and I accept everything that comes out of what we would normally consider a disruptive moment. (5)

———

In every molecule of our bodies we have extra energy that we never use. We only use it in a moment of total danger. I learned how to use that type of energy in front of the audience without having any kind of danger. This is the transition you make from an ordinary-self to a super-self. (7)

———

And while it is true that I can spend hours
on end without speaking, when I finish
I need to shout. (8)

———

Performance is the medium that gave me
the opportunity to set very few, precise rules
that I can only follow as an artist, in both a
given space and time frame. As a human
being, normally I would not have that same
stamina and courage that I have
when I'm performing. (5)

———

When I do performance I get into a state that is different from the state of reality and I become like a receiver and [transmitter] of some other type of energy which is not my own. And this happens every time and it affects me and it affects other people. (9)

———

When I have an idea about a new performative work, I don't think of any potential narrative situations. I have a set of instructions and a defined time for them to unfold. Everything happening in between becomes part of the work and, therefore, its narrative. (5)

———

It took 50 years of my career for people to stop asking me why performance is art, as it is not conventional. People tell you that you are a masochist, a sadist, an exhibitionist, that it is nonsense, not art. Performance art was only watched by your circle of friends. Now there are hundreds of thousands of people watching. [The Artist Is Present was seen by 17 million people on Facebook.] (7)

———

The House with the Ocean View was this long durational performance of 12 days without eating, just observing the audience and living in the gallery. Of course, there was no ocean—the ocean was the public. (10)

———

I've always been impressed by artists who say, "I don't care about the public, I'm just doing this for myself," but for me it has to serve a purpose: it has to communicate a message to people. When you see a good performance, it changes your life. Unfortunately, there are many performances that just annoy you, and that is the problem. (9)

———

In the beginning of early performance practice, there was a group of us at the time that actually thought we should not film at all or document in any possible way. No photographs. Meaning that only what we do then and there exists within the memory of the audience seeing the work and that's it. But, very soon, I understood that actually this is not possible, that I really needed to have documentation and I wanted to kind of save and project for the future how the performances were made. (4)

———

In the 1970s they made great performance work but the lousy documentation makes it look like shit. Whereas you now have great documentation of very bad artworks. The technology has developed so well that everything looks glamorous. But, when you're talking about performance art, if possible you should always show the video material because it is still so much closer to reality than slides. A frozen photograph is just mystification. (10)

———

If you take a piece of music, or you take stuff from a book, you have to pay for it. And you have to acknowledge the composer and the author. But not with a performer. I was so angry with young critics who praised young performance artists doing things as though it was the first time ever when it was done so many times before that. My generation has really been damaged by that. (10)

Performance art has to live and survive. It cannot be put on walls. If we do not perform and recreate it, the art fuckers and the theatre fuckers and the dance fuckers and the film fuckers, and the fashion fuckers, and the MTV fuckers will rip us off without credit even more than they do anyway. (2)

Many artists are absolutely against the re-performance of works. But I'm very willing to give permission for re-performance. Performance is a live form of art, a time-based art, and if it is not re-performed—even without the original artist's charisma, the new performer can bring new charisma, even if the piece is changed—it is still better than mere documentation in books or video. (10)

One of the most beautiful works by Yves Klein in the 1950s was when, on a bridge of the Seine, he sold *The Artist's Sensibility* to his collector. The collector signed a cheque and gave it to the artist, and the artist took a match and burned the cheque and let the ashes fall into the river. So there was a kind of immaterial transmission of the artist's sensibility. This was a wonderful act. (10)

———

I truly believe that long-durational work is the
most important type of work right now.
Because of the way we live, our lives are
getting shorter and shorter, so art has to
get longer and longer. (10)

———

For me, performance is when the performer
steps into his own mental and physical
construction in front of the public. It's a kind
of energy dialogue. They are not rehearsed or
repeated but done once basically. There is a
concept that is a platform for the performer to
follow, but at the same time, he doesn't know
the outcome of the performance in that
moment. It is very different from the theater.
There is a constant dialogue between the
performer and the public. (13)

———

The negative aspect is that after performances, many artists cannot continue because of the amount of effort and energy required. You're permanently exposed to the public, and the artist's nature needs the seclusion of the studio. ... The second thing is the market. There is nothing left over. There is not much except the memory of the audience. (13)

———

During the very restricted, very long-duration works ... you come to a point in which you have a total feeling of harmony, luminosity, clarity. It is a state of happiness, and unconditional love for everything and everybody. ... The moments of synchronicity are incredible—when everything just comes into a kind of balance—and I think that to do that, you really have to work on yourself; it doesn't come easy. (15)

———

[The *Artist Is Present*] was much better if the people sat longer than shorter because there was more time to work with the material, with the energy. When they sit for a short time, it's kind of a short investment and they can't get as much out of it. For me, it's very important that I create the kind of circumstances in the space that when people come into that zone they actually forget about the time. (21)

———

Performance is one of the most transformative forms of art. It never dies, even if at times it seems it has completely disappeared from art practice. It appears again in very unusual ways, and in all its splendor. (20)

———

I am sick and tired of the mistreatment of performance art. (2)

———

I believe performance art is like a phoenix, dying and being reborn from its own ashes over and over again. Every generation has had a different attitude toward performance art and how it should have pushed the limits more. (20)

———

I took all the elements that had helped me and created my own mix and called it "The Abramović Method." I actually just issued a set of cards called "The Abramović Method"; they're playful, but at the same time, people could really be helped by any of these exercises because they've really helped me. I like to share with everybody. (15)

———

I learn from my performances, not my life— because in life I always tend to do what I like and that's kind of a disaster. But in performance I always put a very high task, which I have to complete, and because of the difficulties, I learn in the process, and I really make tremendous change in my private life.

(21)

———

With performance, everything is memory and sensations that you have. Good performance continues to live through narrative, the stories that people tell about the experience. Performance is very fragile and because of that, it's one of the most difficult forms of art there is. I've spent all my life trying to bring performance into the mainstream category.

(22)

———

The last performance is always the one that has the greatest impact on me. I never look back, I always look ahead. (8)

———

Inspirations
and Influences

I expose myself to life, and from that, ideas come as a surprise. I totally dismiss the ones that are pleasant and easy. I'm only interested in the ones that really disturb me and that I get obsessed about. They're what bring me to new territory. (1)

———

I'm interested in nature and people from different cultures who push their bodies and their minds in a way we don't understand. (1)

———

If you do [only] things you like, you never change. There is nowhere to go, you [are] always doing the same things again and again. (19)

———

Coming out of Yugoslavia I did not know about the Beatles or the Rolling Stones—I was listening to Bach, Mozart, Brahms, or Russian composers, so I wasn't really aware of this impulse. (10)

———

It's very important to be vulnerable and to show the things you're afraid and ashamed of to everybody—not just to people you love but also to the public. That way, we have a connection. We create trust. (1)

———

When I am not performing, for instance,
I am really very quiet and ordinary. I don't
drink or smoke and I have never taken drugs.
I am probably the most boring person
you could meet. (2)

———

My work is so hardcore, I put so much
into it and it's really serious, and so when I
come to real life I have to go a different way
completely: I want to have fun, I want to have
ice cream or chocolate. And I love to laugh—
for me, it cures everything. (9)

———

One thing that is really important in an artist's
life is humor. You have to learn to laugh.
In order to do that you need to learn
to laugh at yourself first. (7)

———

For me, the purpose of doing anything is
to lift the human spirit. It's so easy to put the
human spirit down—you can do it in three
seconds—and I'm so fed up with art that
shows how shitty reality is, because we
already know how shitty it is. I want to know
what I can do to change it. Even if it is the
smallest contribution, it's still a contribution.
And if everybody had this kind of idea,
the world would be a different place. (9)

———

To elevate [the] human spirit, that's really
our task, which I think that so many
artists forget to do. (18)

―――――

I always remember a very important thing
about Matisse, the painter. During the Second
World War, when Picasso was painting *Guernica*
and everybody was in a hell of sorts—you
know, painting atrocities and difficult motifs
and war disasters—Matisse, during the
entirety of the Second World War, painted
flowers, only flowers. And if you look at this,
I understand on such a deep spiritual level
that actually, yes, we are in hell, so let's look
into the flowers, let's lift our spirits! This is
what I really feel, and this is what
I wanted my work to be. (15)

―――――

I want to bring young people in afresh so
they can experience the beautiful work of
Beuys, Acconci, Valie Export, and Nauman.
The best way to do that is to bring those
works alive, to perform them. (2)

———

I love this relationship with young people.
To be there for them and offer advice
about the world. (3)

———

A good idea will stand the test of time and
remain invaluable, regardless of technological
advancements. Strong ideas are universal. (4)

———

The awareness that we would not always be here was always something traumatic for me. At that moment I started to work with the notion of death and the importance of thoughts about death to somehow exorcize those fears. This gave rise to the piece *Nude with Skeleton*, to help me come to grips with this idea. (8)

———

We've become consumer junkies, art is a commodity, and just to show people that you are there with nothing and you can do something with that and get a really profound experience is important. (9)

———

This is about me, not about the public. They have never disappointed me; for me, a hundred percent is not enough. I must give my all, 150 percent, and perhaps they will not notice the difference, but they will be there. If I give less, they will leave. (8)

———

I think I all my life trained for this kind of work. I spent a year with Aborigines in Central Australia, I went to deserts, I have for more than 25 years worked with Tibetans in different retreats, all to understand how the mind works and to learn to control it. (9)

———

I had such strong clairvoyant experiences, especially when I went to live with the Aborigines in Central Australia [in 1980–81]. I wrote down the things I saw—in pure daylight—and then I checked them with the newspaper. I predicted an earthquake in Italy [in November 1980] 48 hours before it happened, the shooting of the Pope [in May 1981] 12 hours before it happened, and so much more. It's almost frightening to say it, but I had this ability. (9)

———

Shamanism is something that interests me enormously. I have just finished this movie on shamanism [*The Space In Between*]: I spent four years going to see places of power and people who have certain power and they taught me how to move the wind, how to make the rain. It's all possible! (9)

———

Elements like blood, bones, knives, honey, milk, and wine all have spiritual meanings and not just in the performances. (13)

———

Dealing with pain is an interesting subject. ...
I was always interested in how various ancient
peoples worked with this in ceremonies—the
ritualization of inflicting a large amount of
pain on their bodies—even to the extent of
being clinically dead. ... to confront pain by
taking this kind of risk in order to liberate
yourself from fear and, at the same time, to
enter another state of consciousness. (10)

———

I still have the scars of the cuts [from the
performance Rhythm 0]. It was a little crazy.
I realized then that the public can kill you.
If you give them total freedom, they will
become frenzied enough to kill you. (2)

———

After the performance [of Rhythm 0], I have
one streak of white hair on my head. I [could
not] get rid of the feeling of fear for a long
time. Because of this performance, I know
where to draw the line so as not to
put myself at such risk. (2)

———

My work is always so serious, so demanding,
both physically and mentally, that after doing
the long performances, I need to laugh.
I need humor, I need time to relax. (11)

———

[The] public feels the fear, feels insecurity, feels when you're not there. So you … and [the] public have to actually be there in the same time, in the same space, and to create this energy dialogue. [The] public and the performer complete the work. Performer without public does nothing. (17)

———

For me, art is so many layers of everything together. And the more layers, the more effect it has, because every person can take the one layer they need at that time. (15)

———

But art definitely also has a healing element,
the kind of divine beauty when you see
something in a painting that creates in you
this incredible tranquility and happiness.
It's all possible and I think art can have this
quality, but it is very rare; so much art
just reflects reality as it is. (15)

Martha Graham said one thing that I always liked. She said, "Wherever dancers dance is the holy ground." And I changed it to something else. I said ... that wherever [the] public stands for me is the holy ground, because every single person in the public is important. (17)

———

To be a great artist ... it's like you are obsessed. It's like there is nothing else in your mind until you realize the work and it's this complexity of the intensity that you put into [the] work. (19)

———

You can understand things from life just
by sitting and watching. You can have
thousands of sensations just by looking
at the night skies. (20)

———

In some of my new pieces, when there is
nothing happening I try to take every possible
kind of expectation out of the piece. There is
no beginning, development, and end. It's just
nothing. It's just presence, pure presence. (23)

———

There is something that John Cage always
told me, that you have to go beyond
boredom or behind boredom. (25)

―――――

I see myself as a bridge going to the East to
get the knowledge and going to the West to
transmit it in the form of performance. People
don't go to the temples anymore. They go to
the museums. And to me, performance can be
a great tool to create some kind of platform
for that kind of experience. (23)

―――――

I think the future of performance will definitely go back to sound. And I think that something like noise music is extremely interesting. It's like a new territory. (23)

———

Now there are some things coming up in performance that we don't have words for. They are in between everything. But it's based on sound. It's based on overtones, low vibrations, high vibrations, where they take up the entire space. (23)

———

For my retrospective I was going to take
a magician and invite him along with an
audience. I was going to be in the audience,
and he was going to be onstage with
instructions in his hands. He was going to
read the instructions and ask anybody from
the audience to come onto the stage and be
hypnotized and under hypnosis do any of the
performances of their choice, with me as a
viewer. I could watch all my performances
being done through the hypnosis of
somebody else. (23)

———

[The Marina Abramović Institute] is very important to me: first, to entrust all my experience, all my knowledge, unconditionally, to young artists, but also to be a kind of platform for science, technology, art, and spirituality all together to create this new reality. (9)

———

I just had a 24-page letter from this kid who told me that [the performance 512 *Hours*] had changed his life. He is 11 years old! It's just mind-blowing. (9)

I believe in the spiritual and cosmic energy. Energy comes to you in a way you cannot explain. We are empty transmitters who receive cosmic energy. So I'm spiritual. A sense of humor is so important. The Dalai Lama always starts with a joke. (24)

———

The Creative Process

I don't work in a studio because I don't like to sit in the studio—I do life. Everything I do is life, and ideas come from life. (15)

―――

I've never really had a studio. A studio makes you lazy and comfortable, and you repeat yourself. (1)

―――

I don't go on holidays. I go on research trips to places that don't have Coca-Cola or electricity, away from civilization. (1)

―――

Solitude is extremely important. Away from home, away from studio, away from family, away from friends. (17)

———

There is not just one aspect to my work, there are so many layers: a social aspect, an erotic aspect, a disturbing aspect, a political aspect. (7)

———

In my work, every kind of work I've been doing is really about transformation of one state to another state and learning all the process. (17)

———

In the beginning I was a painter, but the moment I stood in front of the public and expressed my ideas using my body as the object and subject of the work, immediately it was clear that this is my best medium. (1)

———

My early research was really into the physical limits of the body, and now it is into the mental. I think I am much stronger now. People say, "She's become soft!" but, I tell you, running into a wall for an hour is much less difficult than sitting motionless for three months. You see, it's not enough to sit on the chair physically; you have to be in the present with your mind at the same time, so that your entire concentration covers the person who is sitting in front of you. (9)

———

[A] really important thing is that you always
remember to surprise yourself. Never mind
the public. But yourself, you have to surprise.

(17)

———

I never rehearse my performances because if
I did I would never go through with them. It
would be crazy to do it then, I would give up.
I come up with a concept and go in front of
the audience and do it. I count on the energy
from the audience. This kind of energy you
don't have in a private space. Without it,
you get scared and stop. (24)

———

I was never actually interested in violence itself. I like to stage painful situations in front of an audience because we are afraid of pain, mortality, and suffering in our lives. By understanding pain you free yourself of the fear of pain. (7)

————

Danger is important because it brings time to the point of the here and now, to the present. Your mind escapes every single second. Every time we blink there is another thought. So to stop time, to just be in the present, you have to be in an extreme, dangerous situation. That's why I stage situations where I have to do some dangerous things—so that the public and I are in the space at the same time. (23)

————

To be a great artist, the rules are all different.
[It takes] a lot of sacrifice, a burning desire,
being obsessed, being *diseased* by that creativity
that can actually burn you inside. (9)

———

Failure is such a great territory to learn
because if you don't risk, you will never go
anywhere. But risk, you can fail. So to include
failure in your own process of work,
it's essential. (17)

———

The more you fail, the more you understand what caused the failure, and you can make the next piece great. (1)

The title of my biography, which is translated in 22 languages, is *Walk Through Walls*. I am not standing in front of the wall, I am walking through it, and I never give up. (3)

My mother taught me absolute discipline while from my father I learned about heroism and not to be afraid of anybody or anything. Later on, I needed to rebel against everyone and be myself. I took the heroism, discipline, self-control, and spirituality and I started to become interested in Buddhism. A mixture of all these contradictions has been reflected in my work. (7)

———

I am incredibly self-conscious in private, because, you know, am I too fat, or I have too big a stomach, or my knees are not good. But when I am in the public I don't care, because I don't present myself, I present purely the female body, whatever it is: young, not young, I don't care. In private, I'm all issues, like everybody else! (9)

———

What is the definition of "art" you are using when you say your work is art? A lot of your early performances sound like exorcism or exhibitionism. Never exhibitionism! That's a word that the public put on me, but then that means that every ritual in ancient and indigenous cultures is exhibitionism; and it is not. There is a purpose, to open the mind in a certain way. (9)

———

When you do any kind of artwork—or work generally—I think you have to put in an enormous amount of preparation, but the results have to look effortless. That's the magic of it. It really looks like—well, here I am just sitting, what is the big deal? (10)

———

You keep still, not moving, and that's when something really interesting happens. (10)

———

When you are in difficult situations, when you really have to show emotional, political, and physical restraint, humor is the only way out. And that is important. And my work has to be balanced by humor. (11)

———

Being an artist, you can make things from
anything. You can make things from dust.
You have this miracle, possibilities. (17)

———

In the performances, I create a structure in
which I can go far into the physical limits that
a body can take. I don't want to die. That is not
the purpose. I want to experience the edge
and how I can get closer to it. (13)

———

In my own work, in my own life, I don't like pain, but in my work I actually stage the painful situation that I'm going through, and lose it in the front of the public. I see very openly how I deal with that. And if I can go through the pain and free myself from it on the other side, anyone else can do the same. … I become the mirror for the public. I am giving them my own experience that they can use for their own life. Because on the other side of the pain is freedom from the fear of pain. (15)

———

I get an idea in my mind, and if this makes
me afraid, as in, "Oh my God this is amazing,
but I could never could do it," then I will do
it. But if I like it, if it's just okay, I'll dismiss
it. It has to haunt me for many, many
days and months. And then I know
have to do it. (15)

———

When I was working with Ulay, we made this quite interesting experiment—we found a doctor who could hypnotize us. For three months we went to sessions three times a week. ... We asked the doctor not to look through our past lives, but to only have us tell him, under hypnosis, about our new ideas. And we didn't listen to any of the recordings from these sessions for three months. After these three months, we both listened to our recordings, and from the ideas that came out of that hypnotic state we created five performances. One is very well known, *Rest Energy* (1980), with the bow and arrow which we held between each other. It was such a good idea, and we got it out of a hypnotic state, not from sitting in the studio. (15)

The problem with performance art is always how to document it. The moment the audience leave[s], all that is left is in the memory of the audience and in the documentation you take at the time, usually photographs and video. This new augmented reality technique is the closest that you can get to real life. (16)

———

The cosmos is breathing, our planet is breathing, and that's it. We are moving around our axes. And then we are moving around the sun, the sun is moving around the galaxy, the galaxy is rolling around something else. This is why when I did [The] *Artist Is Present*, I didn't need to move. We are moving enough. I said, just be static in one point, be the eye of the tornado. (15)

———

An artist should stay for long periods of time at waterfalls. An artist should stay for long periods of time at exploding volcanoes. An artist should stay for long periods of time looking at fast-running rivers. An artist should stay for long periods of time looking at the horizon where the ocean and sky meet. An artist should stay for long periods of time looking at the stars in the night sky. (17)

———

I think that the public should know about your contradictions, because they can connect with you even more then. (18)

———

I learned so much about my body [during *The Artist Is Present*]. I learned that in your body you have so much space and you can actually move inside that. There is space between organs, there is space between bones, there is space between atom and cell, so you can actually start training yourself to breathe a kind of air into that space. And then I understood that the pain is actually not having space, it's when organs and everything press inside, so by breathing air you can make the pain just disappear. (21)

There is so much secret knowledge being preserved, because pain is like a door. You have to enter through the pain into that other space. That is what all superstition is. That's why Aborigines at ceremonies will literally become clinically dead in order to understand what is behind all these things. Our minds will try everything to mislead us and say, "No no, this is painful. I can't do it." And actually when you understand the pain it doesn't matter anymore. You can do anything. You can stop the pain, you can remove it from your consciousness. (23)

I've developed something over the years called the "Abramović Method." It's a series of restrictions which, when completed, can help attain a sharper stage of consciousness. (24)

———

Every task I set up in front of me I realized from the beginning to the end. Maybe sometimes to the viewer it could look like I'm in a prison of my own ideas, but that prison is my choice. (25)

———

Reflections on Art
and Life

Beauty doesn't have a definition. What is important is what moves you. (20)

———

I really believe that beauty can come from ugliness and disorder and asymmetrical experiences. If we are fixed on the classical idea of beauty, we are missing the point. (14)

———

Even though I was born in a family living in Belgrade, ever since I was a child I've never felt that I belong somewhere. I always think that my family was not a family that I chose— it was given to me for whatever reason. And all I ever wanted to do is leave the country and travel around the world, and see the entire Earth, the planet, as my work studio. (15)

———

I've always wanted to lift the human spirit. And that's mostly been the purpose of my early work, since I was a child. ... It's such a big and important ritual to actually see the potential in every human being, because we all have potential. (15)

––––

Artists have to be free human beings. They have to have the complete freedom to express their ideas with no restrictions. (11)

––––

Intuition is very important—that kind of gut feeling that comes from nowhere. (17)

––––

If you compare artists, spiritual leaders, and scientists, what spiritual leaders and artists have in common is intuition. Scientists need proof of something that spiritual people and artists already know. (15)

———

I think before you understand the concept of my work, you have an emotional reaction to it. To me, that's the right kind of response to art. It has to move you in a certain way. (22)

———

The juxtaposition of good work with the spiritual element is essential: It gives you the depth that you need to understand, and future generations can reuse it again and again. (20)

———

I'm only angry at myself if I know that I didn't give my 120%. But if I give everything, you can criticize, you can ridicule, you can do anything, and it doesn't touch me. (1)

———

You have to believe that you're right, even if everybody believes you are wrong. (1)

———

I hate it when artists from my generation become tired, depressed, and complain about art being dead. It is nonsense. Art is intrinsic to the human being; it is impossible for it to die. (7)

———

Art is like oxygen—we need it. (18)

———

I think that artists have to be erotic and sexual.
They have to love food, life, relationships.
That is what I love about life. (7)

———

The more you think about death, the
more you enjoy life. (8)

———

Let's enjoy this moment before the world
explodes, though I am very worried. (3)

———

Every day I am thinking of death and of how much time I really have left to accomplish what I want to. I want to leave good ideas behind me, because only good ideas have a long life—not material goods, which I'm not attached to. And I show this with how I live my life. (9)

———

I talk about eroticism as a very important part of human life. The primary energy we have is energy for reproduction. The more erotic energy you have, the more you have to give because it can be translated into sexual energy, but it can also become creative and destructive energy. The more energy you have, the more potential you have: the passion to love and to suffer. (22)

———

Love has always been important in my life.
I always fall in love with the wrong people,
I get disappointed, then I do it again. (7)

The best erotic life I have had was after the
menopause. So yes, sexuality is important. (7)

It is up to us how we transform this sexual
energy. It can be transformed through
violence, war, killing, tenderness, love, or
spirituality. It depends how we use that
energy but the fundamental, raw
energy is a sexual one. (7)

People who have only seen my work cannot believe how I am in private life, and people who have only seen me in private life cannot believe the kind of work I'm doing. So, it's a contradiction. And that contradiction is one of the things I am exposing in my work, because all of us have it[,] and if you really show your vulnerability and expose things you are ashamed of especially, you create a different communication based on trust. (9)

———

I don't have secrets. I write about them, and I like to expose to the public. And I like to share with the public. So if I can show you my bullshit, show me your bullshit, then we have real conversation. (17)

———

You get what you get from me. I don't hide anything. There is no dark side, because I tell it all. (9)

————

I'm not pretending. (9)

————

Every human being has contradictions, but we are ashamed to expose them. (17)

————

If some kid says to me, "I would like to be an artist," I tell him right away: "You're not one." Because you can't *like* to be an artist—you are one or you're not. Being an artist is like breathing. If you don't breathe, you die. If you wake up in the morning and you have this urge to create, you are pretty certainly an artist, because, like breathing, it's a necessity.

(9)

———

The deeper you go into yourself, the more original you become. You have to be authentic and love what you are doing. ... You have to be born with an urge to create. (22)

———

I crave truth. This is important, because I have always found that, in many ways in political society, given the way the news goes, the truth is hidden from us. (11)

———

Now, I live in America, where things, I think, are so much more perverse, because things are distorted in complex ways in the name of democracy, and this is not truth either. (11)

———

I really think that art is not democratic,
[it has] never been. (18)

———

Talking about the truth, there are so
many truths and the one thing that is so
important—and I talk from the perspective
of an artist, that is what I am—is that, to not
lie to yourself, that is so important … and not
to repeat yourself, and to not over-produce,
and not to have compromise
with the market. (18)

———

There is nothing wrong with technology, it is our approach that is wrong. We are addicted. We would spend more time playing video games or looking at computers than communicating with another human being. (7)

———

I think this virtual reality is taking over completely, and … science-fiction books become reality more and more. And that's something which is very scary. (18)

———

I always feel that technology is all progress
and all reckless. You become an invalid
without looking at your own abilities. (13)

———

You know so much about a person, without
one word spoken, just by looking at them.
It's really true what they say, that the
eyes are the door of the soul. (9)

———

There is a very interesting Sufi wisdom quote that says, "the worst is the best," and I think we have to learn from that. If we always think that everything is going easy and we take our lives for granted, when some really difficult situations come up, we are unprepared. (15)

———

It is very important to focus on temporality and on the human existence in order to be able to focus on life. (8)

———

We have to see what is our purpose on this planet, and how we can use our time, our one lifetime, to do the best. (15)

———

To me, good art has to have not just one
but many lives. (13)

———

There's a friend of mine, an American critic,
who says, "I hate your work because it always
makes me cry." People want to have an
intellectual response to art, especially the
British, but when I performed *512 Hours*
at the Serpentine Galleries in 2014,
lots of people cried. (22)

———

I really think that for something to be good, it
has to be emotional. ... I have this joke—I say
if a movie doesn't make you cry, the movie
is not good. I need to cry. (15)

———

We are a tiny little dot in the Universe. We are not in the middle of the Milky Way. We are actually in the periphery, a little blue planet that can be hit by an asteroid at any second. ... So if we see it that way—how vulnerable, how incredibly insignificant we are—we should really take our life as a miracle. Every single day is a miracle. (15)

———

We are all little grains of dust in the cosmos. (7)

———

I don't believe in [a] kind of God sitting up there with a beard. But I believe in energy. (17)

———

Bad news, we're all going to die. So it's very important that in one point of your life, you prepare for that exit, so that exit has to be a celebration. (17)

———

My whole work comes to this very simple truth, that actually the only thing we can relate [to] in this moment is now, this moment. (18)

———

An Artist's Life Manifesto by Marina Abramović.
An artist's conduct in his life: An artist should
not lie to himself or others. An artist should
not steal ideas from other artists. An artist
should not compromise for himself or in
regards to the art market. An artist should not
kill another human being. An artist should
not make himself into an idol. (17)

———

The good idea can have many lives.
So, what is this good idea? (18)

———

Joseph Beuys thinks that art can change the world. I don't believe that, but I really think that certain artists can give awareness, can affect society's way of thinking, and can give some good questions to the society, not always the answers. (18)

———

The human being doesn't change easily—we only change with disaster. (18)

———

The mind is the biggest obstacle to everything. (10)

———

The art studios are full of art pollution.
We have really serious art pollution
on this planet. (18)

———

Art has its own life that is detached from the
creator. ... [G]ood art is transcendental,
and it belongs to everybody. (20)

———

Real artists always change their territories
and they go to the land [where] they have
never been and there is unknown territory
and then you can fail or not. (19)

———

I don't care if you are an artist, a shoemaker, or a street cleaner. What's important is understanding who you are. (20)

———

Art should not just raise philosophical questions, but should raise every possible question. (20)

———

The more difficult the situation is, the more we need culture and art to survive. I remember Susan Sontag going to Sarajevo in the time of the Bosnian war and directing *Waiting for Godot* in a bomb shelter. The most important thing is to keep the human spirit up, not down. (25)

———

It has taken me 40 years to put performance into the mainstream. If I really can in any way encourage mindfulness in the young generation, that's a huge, huge plus. Something has to be done to lift the human spirit, and I think I am achieving something. (9)

———

I'm afraid of everything, but with a healthy attitude. Everyone has an expiration date. I remember how Leonard Cohen said, "I'm in the third act." I really feel this is the third act, so I do my best. (24)

———

I don't look to the past. I look to the new work. It's changing all the time. (13)

———

SOURCES

1. Beard, Alison. "Life's Work: An Interview with Marina Abramović." *Harvard Business Review*, November 2016. https://hbr.org/2016/11/marina-abramovi.

2. O'Hagan, Sean. "Interview: Marina Abramović." *The Guardian*, October 2, 2010. https://www.theguardian.com/artanddesign/2010/oct/03/interview-marina-abramovic-performance-artist.

3. Macias, Ernesto. "Marina Abramović Is Forever Young." *Interview*, March 31, 2022. https://www.interviewmagazine.com/art/marina-abramovic-is-forever-young.

4. Estorick, Alex. "An Interview with Marina Abramović." *Right Click Save*, July 11, 2022. https://www.rightclicksave.com/article/an-interview-with-marina-abramovic.

5. Ferrante, Elena. "'I have a lot of questions for you': Elena Ferrante Talks to Marina Abramović." *Financial Times*, September 24, 2021. https://www.ft.com/content/009042c7-efac-4003-a3b1-5945a0cf9270.

6. Wally, Maxine. "The Rebirth of Marina Abramović." *W* magazine, March 15, 2022. https://www.wmagazine.com/culture/marina-abramovic-retrospective-sean-kelly-gallery-exhibition-performative-interview.

7. Cué, Elena. "Interview with Marina Abramović." Alejandra de Argos, November 26, 2018. https://www.alejandradeargos.com/index.php/en/all-articles/21-guests-with-art/41625-marina-abramovic-interview.

8. Peuser, Marcela Costa, and Marina Oybin. "Marina Abramović: 'I like to push the limits, but I love life too much.'" Arte al Día. https://www.artealdia.com/International/Contents/Profiles/Marina_Abramovic_I_like_to_push_the_limits_but_I_love_life_too_much.

9. Sage, Bev, and Huw Spanner. "Pillow Talk: Marina Abramović." High Profiles, October 1, 2014. https://highprofiles.info/interview/marina-abramovic/.

10. Blazwick, Iwona. "The Artist Is Present." *Art Monthly*, September 2011. https://www.artmonthly.co.uk/magazine/site/article/marina-abramovic-interviewed-by-iwona-blazwick-september-2011.

11. Pál, Dániel Levente. "Democracy Has Become Perverse: Interview with Marina Abramović." *Continental Literary Magazine*, April 5, 2022. https://continentalmagazine.com/2022/04/05/democracy-has-become-perverse-interview-marina-abramovic/.

12. Wally, Maxine. "The Rebirth of Marina Abramović." *W* magazine, March 15, 2022. https://www.wmagazine.com/culture/marina-abramovic-retrospective-sean-kelly-gallery-exhibition-performative-interview.

13. Sudbanthad, Pitchaya. "Marina Abramović." *Museo* magazine, 1998. https://www.museomagazine.com /MARINA-ABRAMOVIC.

14. Lentjes, Rebecca. "The Listener Is Present: Marina Abramović on Music." *Van Magazine*, November 22, 2018. https://van-magazine.com/mag/marina-abramovic/.

15. Meistere, Una. "Be the Eye of the Tornado: An Interview with Marina Abramović." Arterritory, February 3, 2022. https://arterritory.com/en/visual_arts/interviews /26017-be_the_eye_of_the_tornado/.

16. Gray, Cat. "Marina Abramović: 'We can't see the pandemic as hopeless, we have to keep our humour.'" *Harper's Bazaar*, October 21, 2020. https://www.harpersbazaar.com/uk /culture/a34427698/marina-abramovic-interview-art -pandemic/.

17. Millman, Debbie. "Design Matters from the Archive: Marina Abramović Performance Artist." SoundCloud, January 25, 2021. https://soundcloud.com/designmatters /design-matters-from-the-archive-marina-abramovic.

18. Erminia Erminia. "Marina Abramović—Interview." October 22, 2017. https://www.youtube.com/watch?v= je-86vaJTUU.

19. "Marina Abramović Interview: Advice to the Young." ouisiana Channel, October 27, 2013. https://www .youtube.com/watch?v=8Ck2q3YgRlY.

20. Marin, Hugo Huerta. *Portrait of an Artist*. New York: Prestel, 2021, 10–29.

21. Stigh, Daniela, and Zoë Jackson. "Marina Abramović: The Artist Speaks." Inside/Out, October 3, 2010. https://www.moma.org/explore/inside_out/2010/06/03/marina-abramovic-the-artist-speaks/.

22. Walton, Millie. "The Performer and Audience Create the Work Together: Marina Abramović." *Trebuchet* magazine, July 25, 2021. https://www.trebuchet-magazine.com/marina-abramovic-interview/.

23. Artspace Editors. "The Fundamentals of Endurance: Marina Abramović on How She Learned to Refuse the Body's Limits and Make Immortal Art." Artspace, September 14, 2016. https://www.artspace.com/magazine/interviews_features/book_report/marina-abramovic-interview-klaus-biesenbach-54182.

24. "An Interview with Marina Abramović." *Barnebys*, December 1, 2018. https://www.barnebys.com/blog/an-interview-with-marina-abramovic.

25. Bria, Ginevra. "Marina Abramović: 'When so much is taken away from us, we have to look at the things directly in front of us.'" *Domus*, March 31, 2020. https://www.domusweb.it/en/art/2020/04/01/marina-abramovi-when-so-much-is-taken-away-from-us-we-have-look-at-the-things-directly-in-front-of-us.html.

26. Sayej, Nadja. "Marina Abramović Wants People to Stop Destroying the Planet." *Observer*, March 17, 2022. https://observer.com/2022/03/marina-abramovic-wants-people-to-stop-destroying-the-planet-interview/.

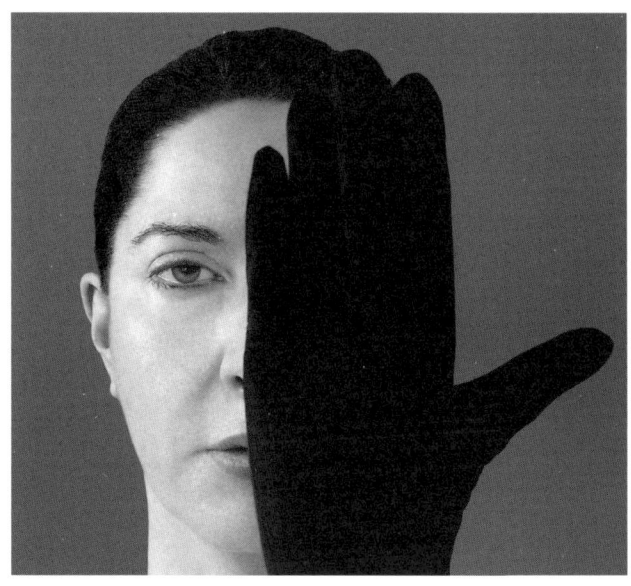

CHRONOLOGY

1946

Marina Abramović is born on November 30 in Belgrade, former Yugoslavia, to an affluent family with politically active parents. Vojo and Danica Abramović, who were Yugoslav partisans during World War II, continue their engagement in General Tito's communist party. Marina spends her first years living with her maternal grandmother, Milica Rosic, who is a devotee of the Orthodox Church. Her early childhood is deeply influenced by her grandmother's faith.

1952

Marina moves in with her parents when her brother Velimir is born. Raising the children is primarily Danica's responsibility; Vojo is largely absent. Life in her parental home under her mother's strict supervision is experienced as difficult and cold. Marina is forced to uphold her mother's compulsive relationship to cleanliness and order.

1953–58

The Abramović family does not celebrate holidays or
   festivals together and rarely expresses their emotions.
   The proximity to art and culture, however, is clear.
   From an early age Marina is encouraged to express
   herself creatively through drawing and painting,
   and at twelve she is given her own studio at home.

1960–65

Marina develops her drawing and painting, often through
   classically figurative floral still lifes and portraits.

1965–70

The young artist studies at the Academy of Fine Arts in
   Belgrade. Her earlier figurative expressions become
   increasingly abstract. Abramović starts painting
   clouds, and the motif recurs in ever-changing forms
   in several of her works from her school years.

1968

Abramović has her first solo exhibition, *Clouds and Their
   Projections*, at the Youth Cultural Centre Gallery in
   Belgrade.

1970–73

During further studies at the Academy of Fine Arts in
Zagreb, Abramović begins to use her body as a tool
in her art and eventually stops painting and drawing.
She spends most of her time at the SKC (Studenski
Kulturni Centar [Student Cultural Center]) in
Belgrade, founded by Tito. She starts experimenting
with sound environments and performance.

1971

Abramović marries the conceptual artist Neša Paripović.

1973

Abramović meets the artist Joseph Beuys in Edinburgh
and later that year at the SKC in Belgrade.
She collaborates with the artist Hermann Nitsch. The
same year, she enacts the performance piece *Rhythm
10* at the Villa Borghese, Museo d'Arte Contempo-
ranea in Rome. The piece is the first of five performances in the *Rhythm* series, in which she explores
the limits of the body and consciousness.

1974

At SKC Abramović performs the work *Rhythm 5*. *Rhythm 4* is presented at the Galleria Diagramma in Milan; *Rhythm 2* is presented at the Gallery of Contemporary Art, Zagreb; *Rhythm 0* is presented at Studio Morra in Naples. Abramović is awarded the "7 Sekretar Skoja" from Galleria Nova, Zagreb, Croatia, for *Rhythm 5*.

1975–76

Abramović travels to Amsterdam to participate in an international gathering for performance artists and meets the German artist Ulay (Frank Uwe Laysiepen, b. 1943). Abramović performs *Role Exchange*.

With the intention of contending with her identity and past, Abramović returns to Belgrade for a series of performance pieces—*Freeing the Voice*, *Freeing the Memory*, and *Freeing the Body* at the SKC. *Art Must Be Beautiful*, *Artist Must Be Beautiful* is performed at the Art Festival Charlottenburg in Copenhagen and *Lips of Thomas* at Galerie Krinzinger, Innsbruck.

1976

Abramović divorces Paripovic, flees her family home, and moves in with Ulay in Amsterdam.

Abramović and Ulay create a number of works under the shared title *Relation Works*. They write the manifesto *Art Vital*, which sets the course for their artistic practice.

Abramović and Ulay perform together for the first time in *Relation in Space* at the Venice Biennale.

1977–79

Abramović and Ulay conceptualize and perform works from the *Relation Works* series.

1979

Abramović and Ulay travel to Sydney, Australia, on the invitation of the 3rd Biennale of Sydney: *European Dialogue*. They present their performance *The Brink*.

The couple get a loft in Amsterdam and come to play a central role in the artistic life of the city.

1980

Abramović and Ulay begin experimenting with
  hypnosis to search in and explore the subconscious.
  They develop the *Self* series, which includes the
  performances *Point of Contact*, *Rest Energy*, *Nature of
  Mind*, and *Timeless Point of View*.
From 1980 onward, Abramović and Ulay work with
  video and photography parallel to their performative
  practice.

1980–81

After receiving a grant from the Australian ministry of
  arts and culture, they travel to Australia and its Great
  Victoria Desert, where they live with the Pitjantjatjara
  tribe and Pintupi tribe for nine months. Influenced
  by Aboriginal culture, they create the performance
  Nightsea Crossing. It is shown for the first time at the
  Art Gallery of New South Wales in Sydney.

1981–86

Nightsea Crossing is performed in cities such as Kassel
  at Documenta 7, Cologne, Düsseldorf, Berlin,

Amsterdam, Chicago, Toronto, Helsinki, Middelburg, Ushimado, São Paulo, New York City, and Lyon.

1981
During their time in Australia, Abramović and Ulay develop the series *Modus Vivendi*.

1982
In order to practice the meditation technique Vipassana, Abramović and Ulay travel to Bodh Gaya, India, where they meet the Dalai Lama and receive teachings from his mentor and teacher, the tulku Ling Rinpoche. They receive Buddhist teachings from Lama Zopa Rinpoche and Lama Thubten Yeshe. They travel to Rajasthan and the Thar Desert in Northwest India and spend time with nomadic tribes.

1983
Abramović and Ulay invite the Tibetan lama Ngawang Soepa Lueyar and the Aboriginal medicine man Charlie Watuma Taruru Tjungurrayi, their travel companion in the Great Victoria Desert, to perform a new

version of *Nightsea Crossing* together. For four days,
the performance piece *Nightsea Crossing Conjunction* is
hosted at the Fodor Museum in the Netherlands.
Abramović and Ulay create the work for video and stage,
Anima Mundi and *Positive Zero*.

1985

Abramović travels to Dharamsala in India. She and Ulay
enact their first play, *Modus Vivendi*, in Bern, Arnhem,
and Baltimore. In collaboration with director Michael
Laub and Mr. Mondo, Abramović and Ulay premiere
Fragilissimo at the Stedelijk Museum in Amsterdam
and the Moderna Museet in Stockholm.

1986

The couple take their first trip to China. Ever since the
trip to the Australian desert in 1980, they have been
working on an idea about a performance-walk along
the Great Wall of China. They apply for support from
the Chinese authorities but are turned down.

1987

Though they have almost entirely broken off their
    personal relationship, Abramović and Ulay continue
    working together. They travel to China again and
    apply again for permission to conduct their walk.
Der Mond, Die Sonne is performed at the Centre d'Art
    Contemporain in Geneva.

1988

After years of preparation, the walk along the Great Wall
    of China begins as the work *The Lovers*. Abramović
    walks from the Shanhai Pass at the wall's east end.
    From the wall's western end near the Gobi Desert,
    Ulay walks in the opposite direction. After ninety
    days, and covering 2,500 kilometers (about 1,550
    miles) each, they meet.
The reunion marks a definitive end to their romantic
    relationship and their twelve-year-long artistic
    collaboration. Abramović and Ulay part ways and
    start to work on their own.

1989

Abramović presents and develops her new solo works, a
series known as *Transitory Objects*. Among other places,
these works are displayed at Oxford's Museum of
Modern Art, Städtische Kunsthalle in Düsseldorf,
and Montreal's Museum of Modern Art.

The Lovers is exhibited at the Stedelijk Museum in
Amsterdam and the Museum van Hedendaagse
Kunst in Antwerp.

Abramović develops the concept of the workshop *Cleaning the House*, a series of exercises aiming to purify
the body and the mind through concentration and
presence.

1990

She's invited to participate in the exhibition *Magiciens de la Terre* at the Centre Pompidou, curated by Jean Hubert
Martin. *The Lovers* opens at the same museum.

Abramović performs *Dragon Heads* at the Museum of
Modern Art in Oxford.

1991

Abramović becomes a guest professor at the Hochschule der Künst in Berlin and at the Académie des Beaux-Arts in Paris. She travels to Brazil a number of times to continue her work on *Transitory Objects*.

1992–93

In Hamburg, Abramović becomes a professor at the Hochschule für Bildende Künste.

Abramović returns to the theater. The autobiographical play *The Biography*, directed by Charles Atlas, premieres in Madrid and is also shown at Documenta 9 in Kassel, the Hebbel Theatre in Berlin, and Kunsthalle Wien in Vienna.

1994

Abramović and Charles Atlas travel to Belgrade to work on the forthcoming play *Delusional*, which is also based on Abramović's life.

1995

The performance *Cleaning the House* is staged at the Sean Kelly Gallery in New York.

A retrospective exhibition, *Marina Abramović: Objects Performance Video Sound*, opens at Oxford's Museum of Modern Art and later at the Irish Museum of Modern Art in Dublin.

1996

Abramović performs *The Onion*, *The Space In Between*, and *Image of Happiness* for video.

1997

Abramović is invited to represent Serbia and Montenegro at the Yugoslavian pavilion at the Venice Biennale but breaks off the collaboration after a conflict with the Montenegrin minister of culture. The performance piece *Balkan Baroque* is shown instead at the Italian pavilion, curated by Germano Celant. Abramović is awarded the Golden Lion prize for Best Artist of the Biennale. The same year, she meets the artist Paolo Canevari, and they begin a romantic relationship.

Abramović performs *Spirit House* for video, consisting of the performances *Insomnia*, *Luminosity*, *Dissolution*, *Lost Souls*, and *Dozing Consciousness*.

1998

Abramović becomes a professor at Hochschule für Bildende Künste in Braunschweig, Germany.

1999

In Mundgod, India, Abramović choreographs a performance with Tibetan monks for the Festival of Sacred Music.

Abramović creates the video installation *The Waterfall* with 120 monks.

2000–2001

Abramović's father, Vojo, dies. The next year the video piece *The Hero*, dedicated to her father, is produced. The interactive project *Dream House* opens in conjunction with Echigo-Tsumari Art Triennial in Japan, where it is permanently installed.

2002

Abramović and Canevari move to New York, and *The House with the Ocean View* is presented at the Sean Kelly Gallery in New York. In front of visitors, Abramović spends twelve days strictly fasting and performing seemingly simple, everyday tasks.

2004

The Art Institute of Chicago gives Abramović an honorary doctorate. She travels to Belgrade to develop the video project *Balkan Erotic Epic* and also participates in the 2004 biennial at the Whitney Museum of American Art in New York.

The Biography Remix, is performed at the Fondazione Roma Europea in Rome and at the Avignon Festival, and *Virgin Warrior/Warrior Virgin* is performed at the Palais de Tokyo in Paris.

2005

Seven Easy Pieces is presented at the Guggenheim Museum in New York.

2006

Abramović and Canevari marry in New York. Abramović buys an estate in Hudson that becomes her private residence and a meeting place for performance artists.

2007

Abramović's mother, Danica, dies in Belgrade.

2009

In the kitchen of an abandoned Carthusian monastery in Spain, Abramović creates a series of video and photographic artworks titled: *The Kitchen: Homage to Saint Theresa*.

2010

The Museum of Modern Art in New York presents the retrospective *The Artist Is Present* with many re-performances of Abramović's works. The artist herself performs the new and demanding piece *The Artist Is Present* for the duration of the exhibition.

2011

The biographical play *The Life and Death of Marina Abramović*, premieres at the Manchester International Festival and tours in Antwerp, Basel, Amsterdam, and Madrid.

2012

Abramović founds the Marina Abramović Institute (MAI), a nonprofit foundation for performance art that focuses on performance, long-durational works, and the use of the "Abramović Method."

The exhibition *Marina Abramović, Balkan Stories* is shown at Kunsthalle Wien, while the documentary *Marina Abramović: The Artist Is Present* premieres at the Sundance Film Festival and participates at the Berlin Film Festival, where it receives the Berlin Film Festival Panorama Audience Award.

2013

Abramović creates the set construction and co-choreographs Ravel's *Bolero*, marking her first collaboration with dancers and choreographers Damien Jalet and Sidi Larbi Cherkaoui.

The Life and Death of Marina Abramović is performed at the Park Avenue Armory in New York.

2014

The exhibition *512 Hours* is presented at London's Serpentine Gallery.

2015

The two exhibitions *Terra Comunal/Communal Land* and
   Private Archaeology open at SESC Pompéia in São Paulo
   and the Museum of Old and New Art in Tasmania,
   respectively. The Abramović Method is presented in
   Sydney as part of the Kaldor Public Art Projects.
In New York, Abramović collaborates with Igor Levitt
   on the work *Goldberg*, performed at the Park Avenue
   Armory.
Abramović is a TED Talks speaker in Vancouver, Canada:
   An Art Made of Trust, Vulnerability and Connection.

2016

Abramović's book *Walk Through Walls: A Memoir* is
   published in twenty-six languages worldwide.
The Space In Between, a film about Abramović's experiences
   in Brazil, premieres at the SXSW Film Festival in
   Austin, Texas, and is screened internationally.

2017–20

Marina Abramović—The Cleaner opens at the Moderna Museet in Stockholm and travels to six museums across

Europe, including the Museum of Contemporary Art in Belgrade.

2018

With Opera Ballet Vlaanderen, Abramović presents *Pelléas et Mélisande* in collaboration with Damien Jalet and Sidi Larbi Cherkaoui.

Abramović travels to Bhutan.

2019

A group of Abramović's *Standing Structures* from the series *Transitory Objects for Human Use* are installed at the Crystal Bridges Museum of American Art in Bentonville, Arkansas. The work is permanently installed in the outdoor sculpture garden.

2020

Abramović premieres her opera *7 Deaths of Marina Callas* at the Bayerische Staatsoper in Munich, Germany.

Abramović is the first artist to take over Sky Arts

television, curating a six-plus-hour program on performance art.

Abramović's work *The Life*, made using augmented reality, is presented at Frieze Los Angeles.

2021

Marina Abramović: That Self/Our Self opens at the Kunsthalle Tübingen in Germany.

2023

Abramović opens her show at the Royal Academy of Arts in London, becoming the first female artist in the institution's 250-year history to occupy the entire gallery space.

Abramović is promoted to Commander of the Order of Arts and Letters in France.

Abramović publishes *A Visual Biography* and *Nomadic Journey and Spirit of Places*.

ACKNOWLEDGMENTS

First, my gratitude and thanks go to Marina Abramović, whose deep insight and iconic artistic presence comprise the foundation of this book. It is truly an honor and a blessing to be aligned with such a powerful mind and creative spirit.

My sincere thanks go to Hugo Huerta Marin, Cathy Koutsavlis, Ellen Holdorf, and the entire team at Marina Abramović's studio for their dedication and valued assistance throughout this project. My thanks as well to Marcello Dantas.

My sincere appreciation, as always, to the entire team at Princeton University Press, especially Michelle Komie, Christie Henry, Terri O'Prey, Jacqueline Poirier, Colleen Suljic, Laurie Schlesinger, Cathy Felgar, Jodi Price, Kathryn Stevens, Cathy Slovensky, and Annie Miller. We remain extremely grateful to PUP for their continued professionalism, encouragement, and passion for our projects together throughout the years.

Thanks as well to Greg Hilty, Alex Logsdail, and the team at Lisson Gallery for their incredible representation and support for Marina and her artwork.

Very special thanks to Taliesin Thomas for her invaluable research on this project, and to editorial director Fiona Graham for her organization of the ISMs series. My thanks as well to Susan Delson for her insightful editorial assistance.

My sincere thanks to Karen Lautanen for her organization aid on this project and many others, and to Steven Rodríguez for his continued support.

Finally, I give all my bottomless gratitude to my amazing wife, Abbey, and to my wonderful children, Justin, Ethan, Ellie, and Jonah for their love and encouragement.

As always, I give endless love and thanks to my mother Judith.

LARRY WARSH

Since the beginning of her career in Belgrade during the early 1970s, **Marina Abramović** has pioneered performance art, creating some of the form's most important early works. Exploring her physical and mental limits, she has withstood pain, exhaustion, and danger in her quest for emotional and spiritual transformation.

Abramović was awarded the Golden Lion for Best Artist at the 1997 Venice Biennale. In 2010, Abramović had her first major US retrospective and simultaneously performed for more than seven hundred hours in *The Artist Is Present* at the Museum of Modern Art in New York. Abramović founded the Marina Abramović Institute (MAI), a platform for immaterial and long-durational work to create new possibilities for collaboration among thinkers of all fields. Her book *Walk through Walls: A Memoir*, was published in 2016.

Larry Warsh has been active in the art world for more than thirty years as a publisher and artist-collaborator. An early collector of Keith Haring and Jean-Michel Basquiat, Warsh was a lead organizer for the exhibition *Basquiat: The Unknown Notebooks*, which debuted at the Brooklyn Museum, New York, in 2015, and later traveled to several American museums. He has loaned artworks by Haring and Basquiat from his collection to numerous exhibitions worldwide, and he served as a curatorial consultant on *Keith Haring | Jean-Michel Basquiat: Crossing Lines* for the NGV. The founder of *Museums Magazine*, Warsh has been involved in many publishing projects and is the editor of several other titles published by Princeton University Press, including Jean-Michel Basquiat's *The Notebooks* (2017), *Keith Haring: 31 Subway Drawings* (2021), and two books by Ai Weiwei, *Humanity* (2018) and *Weiwei-isms* (2012). Warsh has served on the board of the Getty Museum Photographs Council and was a founding member of the Basquiat Authentication Committee until its dissolution in 2012.

ILLUSTRATIONS

Frontispiece: Portrait of Marina Abramović. Photo by Dow Wasiksir, 2023.

Page 140: Marina Abramović, *Light Side/Dark Side*, 2006. Silver gelatin print. © Marina Abramović. Courtesy of the Marina Abramović Archives.

ISMs

Larry Warsh, Series Editor

The ISMs series distills the voices of an exciting range of visual artists and designers into captivating, beautifully made books of quotations for a new generation of readers. In turn passionate, inspiring, humorous, witty, and challenging, these collections offer powerful statements on topics ranging from contemporary culture, politics, and race, to creativity, humanity, and he role of art in the world. Books in this series are edited by Larry Warsh and published by Princeton University Press in association with No More Rulers.

Abramović-isms, Marina Abramović

JR-isms, JR

Holzer-isms: Artist's Edition, Jenny Holzer

Neshat-isms, Shirin Neshat

Judy Chicago-isms, Judy Chicago

Pharrell-isms, Pharrell Williams